HANDS-ON GRAMMAR

Multimodal Grammar and Language Mini Lessons

GRADES 5-12

Katherine S. McKnight

.

DEDICATION

For Jim, Ellie, and Colin, who bring joy to my life;

and

for Mary, my sister foremost, and writing teacher extraordinaire.

CONTENTS

ACKNOWLEDGMENTS

My first teacher was my mom, Patricia Siewert. She was also a teacher in the Chicago Public Schools for over three decades, and always reminded me that teaching is an act of love and social justice. Her teaching spirit is always in every book that I write for fellow educators. My sister, Mary, was often my writing coach when I would get stuck or discouraged. She passed away suddenly as I was writing this book, and her words of wisdom and writing advice are sorely missed. A teacher in her own right, Mary was the head of the writing program at Second City in Chicago, and her legacy is her uncanny ability to build confidence and skill in those who desired to write. Finally, I need to thank my colleague and friend, Warren Thomas Rocco, who designed the cover for this book, and cheered me on as I cobbled together this teacher resource.

HOW TO USE THIS BOOK

I have always been intimidated by grammar, let alone teaching it. Like so many other teachers, I learned grammar through big grammar books that stated important definitions like, "a noun is a person, place, thing, or idea" and "a verb is an action word." As a high school student, I struggled to learn how to apply these definitions to multiple choice-based assessments. Most of the time, it didn't make sense to me as my teachers would say things like, "You have to learn grammar for college and to be a better writer." While I certainly don't disagree with what my teachers advised me over twenty years ago, I do disagree that learning grammar through a big book and isolated multiple choice exercises didn't make me a better writer. I actually became a more tense and frightened writer. I was afraid of making stupid and frequent mistakes. As I progressed through my teacher preparation program after I graduated with my Bachelor of Arts in American Civilization, I learned that teaching grammar in isolation didn't work. Grammar and writing mechanics must be taught within the context of writing. I gobbled up advice from Nancie Atwell and Linda Reif as I valiantly worked on developing adolescent writers who used grammar knowledge to become better writers. There was some success with my efforts, but I often did not witness a seamless transition between grammar knowledge and student writing. I knew that I was screwing it up and needed to find some solution so that my students would make the connection between more abstract grammatical concepts and more concrete writing experiences. Where would I find a solution to my teaching turmoil? Little did I know, the solution would be found in my math teacher colleagues' teaching.

Oftentimes, math teachers use physical models to demonstrate and explain abstract concepts. I wondered if I could do the same to teach grammar. Like math, grammar is abstract for most adolescents. I started to explore manipulatives for the teaching of grammar and I looked to Howard Gardner's theory of multiple intelligences as a means to teach grammar to my students. As I tinkered with these grammar models, I saw a change in my students. Teaching my students about apostrophes, subject/verb agreement, and nouns changed. During this period of discovery, my students and I began to understand that learning about grammar was actually about learning how to manipulate and use language to become more effective writers.

This book contains forty grammar and language mini lessons that incorporate kinesthetic models and Gardner's theory of multiple intelligences. As you look through the lessons and consider which lessons to use with your students, there are a few things to remember and know about writing and grammar mini lessons:

Determine Content Need: If the students need to learn how to use commas, it might be appropriate for a seventh-grade student to learn about each of the seven comma rules in a series of seven separate mini lessons. If you are teaching about the seven comma rules to twelfth-graders, we would hope that all of rules could be covered in one mini lesson that reviews this material.

Keep Them Short: The whole point of grammar and mini lessons is to break down concepts into small, digestible chunks. Any mini lesson that is more than ten minutes in length, is too long. If you have a mini lesson that is ten minutes or more, it is time to review the content and revise.

Make Them Simple: Mini lessons are most effective when the grammar or writing concept is the smallest digestible chunk. Covering common nouns, proper nouns, and collective nouns in one lesson may be too much. Cover each type of noun in a separate mini lesson.

Engage Students and Provide for Interaction: Now, more than ever before, we have to discover highly engaging and interesting instructional experiences for our technologically savvy students. Our twenty-first-century students have unlimited access to information at any time. Our classrooms must provide this hands-on experience that resembles the "real world."

Provide Practice Time: Before students are ready to transfer what they learn about grammar and writing into their personal writing, they need practice. In general, teach the concept, allow for practice, and the third stage, which is the most important, is transference to individual writing.

Consider, What's Next?: If the students understand common nouns, proper nouns, and collective nouns, it is probably time to teach about apostrophes, or adjectives.

Evaluate: The best way to assess whether the students understand the grammatical and writing concepts that were taught is to determine whether the students have applied them to their writing. Writing rubrics or checklists that list the successful application of grammatical and writing concepts will help you to monitor individual mastery.

As with all classroom activities, it is extremely helpful for all of the students when you provide both verbal and written directions. Written directions can be on a sheet of paper with each poster board, or simply write the directions on the board or overhead.

As I learned how to develop grammar and writing lesson that actively involve multiple intelligences, I noticed that my students were better internalizing what I was teaching. I had far greater success in teaching students about grammar and writing than I did using worksheets and grammar books.

LESSON ONE: Action Contractions

Overview and Tips for Classroom Implementation

Students, especially English Language Learners (ELL), often do not understand that the apostrophe mark in a contraction like *can't* or *wouldn't* actually signals to the reader that there are letters missing. In this activity the students pair puzzle pieces to create contractions. I often taught this mini lesson at the beginning of class.

Step-by-Step Lesson Instructions

Step One: Use 4 x 6 index cards and write the words that make up the contraction on one side and the contraction on the other side of the index card. You can use the table (figure 1) as a resource.

Step Two: Distribute one puzzle piece per student. Once the students have a puzzle piece, instruct the students to find the matching puzzle piece.

Step Three: Once the students are correctly paired, have the students create a single line or a circle so that they can see all of the contractions. Discuss with the students the different contractions.

Additional Tips

When I conduct this mini lesson in the classroom, I like to use it as an opening activity. When the students enter the classroom at the beginning of the class period, I hand each of them a puzzle piece. While I take attendance the students need to find their contraction pair and line up. It is also especially helpful for the students if I create the puzzle pieces on matching color paper. It makes it easier to find the paired piece and it also allows the students to do a quick check to ensure that their contraction is correct. For example, the students know that if they have a red piece, they need to pair with a student who has a red puzzle piece; if a student has a blue puzzle piece, they pair with a blue piece, and so on.

Figure 1: Words and Contractions

WORDS	CONTRACTION
is +not	isn't
are +not	aren't
was +not	wasn't
were +not	weren't
have +not	haven't
has +not	hasn't
had +not	hadn't
will +not	won't
would +not	wouldn't
do +not	don't
does +not	doesn't
did +not	didn't
can + not	can't
could +not	couldn't
should +not	shouldn't
might +not	mightn't
must + not	mustn't

WORDS	CONTRACTION
I + am	I'm
I + will	I'll
I + had	I'd
you+ are	you're
you + will	you'll
you+ would	you'd
you+ have	you've
he+ is	he's
he+ will	he'll
he + would	he'd
he+ has	he's
he+ had	he'd
she + is	she's
she+ will	she'll
she + would	she'd
she+ has	she's
she+ had	she'd

LESSON TWO: Adjectives Abound

Overview and Tips for Classroom Implementation

Adding descriptive language in student writing can be challenging. This mini lesson incorporates strong visuals to prompt students to use adjectives and to develop skills for incorporating figurative language in narrative writing.

Step-by-Step Lesson Instructions

Step One: Collect pictures from different kinds of sources. Allow the students to work in pairs for this mini lesson. The students can select pictures from your collection.

Step Two: Instruct the students to record all of the adjectives that they could use to describe the selected picture. Give the students three minutes to complete the list. Use a timer as the students work on this part of the mini lesson.

Step Three: Once the students have completed the list, instruct them to use a thesaurus to add to the list.

Step Four: Using the completed adjective list, the student pairs can write a narrative paragraph about the picture. The students can also attach the picture that they used to the list that they created.

Additional Tips

I scour bookstores, used bookstores, and garage sales for pictures. Old coffee table books contain better photos for this activity rather than those that come from magazines or are printed from the Internet. Although it's tough for me to disassemble books, I do it and use the pictures for this activity. This activity is also more effective when you do not use pictures of famous people or events. Use pictures of nature, locations, buildings, and everyday people.

LESSON THREE: Adjective Carousel

Overview and Tips for Classroom Implementation

This lesson creates the opportunity to generate lists of adjectives that will develop students' word knowledge. Prompting the student writer to go beyond the most commonly used adjectives, the adjective carousel activity generates lists of adjectives that the student writer can use as a reference at a later date.

Step-by-Step Lesson Instructions

Step One: Begin by putting students in groups of three or four. Give each group a sheet of newsprint, chart paper, or large construction paper. Each group's sheet has a different adjective written on it. One student in each group can be the recorder and is a given a specific Magic Marker color. (Each group recorder has a different color Magic Marker so that at the end of the activity, you will know which group recorded the information on each chart paper.)

Step Two: Instruct the students that they will be given thirty seconds to write down on their chart paper all of the synonyms that they can think of for the adjective listed on the chart paper. Also explain to the students that when time is called, they will pass their chart paper to the next group. The new group will add even more synonyms for the adjective listed on the chart paper. These exchanges will continue until every group has contributed synonyms to every adjective chart.

Additional Tips

After the second exchange, the groups will need additional times. On the third exchange, extend the time to 40 seconds, then 50 seconds, and so on until all of the groups have contributed to each adjective chart. I also suggest that on the last rotation that you give the students about 2-3 minutes so that they can add synonyms that they can find through an outside source like a thesaurus. It is also a good idea to post the students' adjective charts with the recorded synonyms in the classroom or a student can also type them up and they can become resource pages for a students' writing folder.

A final tip: start with common adjectives like colors, sizes, or that are concept related. It will be easier for the students to generate the lists. For older and more proficient students, choose adjectives that may be more geared toward college readiness. Students will need more time to talk about and think of other terms to be added to the brainstorm list. Keep having students brainstorm, write, and pass until each group has had a chance to add ideas to each of the subtopic sheets. Let them pass it the final time to the group who had each sheet first.

LESSON FOUR: Apostrophes in Public

Overview and Tips for Classroom Implementation

One of my favorite classroom incentives for students when they are developing writing and grammar skills is to encourage them to find usage errors and confusing language on signs and other printed media. They are usually astounded at the number of errors that they find in printed media. In this mini lesson, I have collected a number of printed media examples where there are errors in apostrophe usage. This kind of mini lesson is not exclusive to apostrophes; you can use any kind of example that has a usage error.

The samples are from signs that I have seen around my neighborhood.

Step-by-Step Lesson Instructions

Step One: Distribute a variety of pictures and printed media examples to the students. I like to have the students in pairs for this activity, but the student groups can be as many as four members.

Step Two: Use the accompanying graphic organizer for this assignment. Students should use the pictures or printed media examples and identify the error and explain why it is incorrect.

Additional Tips

One of the essential elements of language learning, at any age, is that the examples are authentic. Through the use of examples that are found in the real world, the language learning experiences are grounded in authenticity. The students also develop a greater awareness of how language is used in the "real world." The graphic organizer can be used as a formative assessment to determine if the students are internalizing the formation of contractions.

Here are some websites that features pictures and text with apostrophe errors.

www.sharoncolon.com/pictures.htm
www.apostropheabuse.com

Figure 2: Public Apostrophe Graphic Organizer

Name_____

Directions: Using the distributed pictures, complete the following information in this graphic organizer:

Picture (Write down the sentence, statement, or signage with the apostrophe error.)	Explain why this is an apostrophe error.	Fix It! Write sentence or statement using the apostrophe correctly.

LESSON FIVE: Applicable Appositive

Overview and Tips for Classroom Implementation

An appositive is a noun or a pronoun that is placed beside a noun pronoun to explain or identify it. This activity can be used as an introduction to appositives or for review.

Step-by-Step Lesson Instructions

Step One: Group the students into pairs. Instruct the students to make a list of five things that they learned about their partner.

Step Two: Instruct the students to create appositive phrases about their partner. You can use the following examples for the students:

Katie, *the English teacher,* tries to make grammar lessons engaging.

Snoopy, *a famous dog*, is a lovable cartoon character.

(Note that the appositive phrases in the examples are in *italics.*)

Step Three: Once the students have completed the sentences with appositive phrases, invite the students to read these out loud and introduce their partners to the whole class.

Additional Tips

This lesson is particularly useful at the beginning of the school year, when the students are getting to know each other. It is also helpful for the teacher to model sentences with appositive phrases for the students.

LESSON SIX: The Colon

Overview and Tips for Classroom Implementation

In this mini lesson, students will learn how to effectively use colons in writing. The colon is a useful punctuation mark for more complicated writing and to cue the audience when additional information is about to be introduced.

Step-by-Step Lesson Instructions

Step One: Introduce the following information about colons to the students.

A colon (:) is a punctuation mark that is used to introduce a series of items. Some reminders about colons:

A colon should not follow directly after a verb or preposition.

Example: The winter months are: December, January, and February.

Use a colon after the salutation of a business letter.

Example: Dear Professor:

Use a colon between the hour and the minute of time.

School starts at 8:00 a.m.

Use a colon between a title and subtitle:

Example: Frankenstein: or, the Modern Prometheus.

Step Two: Write the following phrases in the table on heavy paper or card stock. The print should be large enough for all of the students to see in class. Note that the colons are missing (for now).

Did you go

to the store

at 5 00 p.m?

The following students

Tayesha, Will, and Sophie

for the spelling bee.

My friend gave me the book,

Frankenstein: or the Modern Prometheus

to read.

In addition to the above phrase cards, make cards with a colon punctuation mark. It is especially helpful to make the colon punctuation cards a different color than the phrase cards.

Step Three: Assign the students into groups of four. Each student will be given a phrase card and a punctuation card. Each group of four students should have four phrase cards and punctuation cards that will make a full sentence that includes a colon punctuation mark.

Step Four: Instruct the students to arrange the phrase cards and punctuation cards in a complete sentence. Once the students have completed the sentence, have each group present it to their classmates.

Additional Tips

For this activity, it is useful to post the colon rules at the front of the room so that the students have an easily accessible reference. Also consider using different colors for the phrase cards and colon punctuation mark cards. Using different colors helps the students to arrange the cards into a cogent sentence.

LESSON SEVEN: Comma—an Overview

Overview and Tips for Classroom Implementation

Commas are tough to teach and tough to master. Even English teachers can occasionally misuse a comma. This lesson provides an overview of the basic rules for commas. I suggest that this lesson be used as an introduction or a quick review, since it is comprehensive.

Step-by-Step Lesson Instructions

Step One: Make copies of the "Ten Quick Comma Rules" (see figure 3 on adjoining page) for the students. I suggest that the students paste a copy into their writing or class notebook. Using poster boards or large sheets of construction paper, write each of the following quick comma rules. There are many more comma rules, but these ten rules are important for student writers to understand.

Each rule will be written on a separate poster board or sheet of construction paper:

Use commas to separate items in a list or series (words, phrases, and clauses).

Example: Colin enjoys *trains, cars,* and *Dr. Seuss.*

Use a comma after the words *yes* or *no* when these are used to start a sentence.

Example: *Yes,* I would like some dessert.

Use a comma before and after a consecutive introductory prepositional phrase.

Example: *At the end of the day in Chicago,* people rush home from work.

Use a comma after an introductory participle or participial phrase.

Example: *Inspired by the professor's comments,* Ellie decided to go to law school.

Use a comma after an introductory adverb clause.

Example: *Before we boarded the airplane,* we needed to pass through security.

Use a comma to separate two or more adjectives that are placed before a noun.

Example: My Girl Scout troop is a *dedicated, kind* group.

Use a comma to separate independent clauses joined by the conjunctions *for, and, nor, but, or,* and *yet.*

Example: Troop 320 wanted to go camping, *but* it was too cold to sleep in tents.

Use a comma to cue a word or words in direct address.

Example: *Jim*, can you reach the top shelf?

Use a comma to cue a parenthetical expression like *such as, I believe,* and *for example.*

Example: This, *I believe*, is the best way to solve the problem.

Use a comma at the beginning and end of an appositive phrase.

Example: Susan, *my dear friend*, likes to kayak.

Step Two: Divide the students into ten groups. Assign each group a different comma rule.

Step Three: Instruct the students to read the assigned comma rule and the example. Provide the following directions:

Provide additional examples that demonstrate your understanding of your assigned comma rule. This is a timed activity, and you will have two minutes to write your example on the poster board.

When time is called, you will pass your poster board to the next group. When your group receives the new comma rule, you will add a new example. This process will repeat until every group has written examples for each of the ten comma rules.

Step Four: Once the students have written examples for each of the ten comma rules, the student groups should check for accuracy the examples for the rule that they were originally assigned.

Additional Tips

Give each group a different color marker so it is easier for you to keep track of which examples belong to which student group. You may have to vary time depending on how the students are working on the examples.

Figure 3: Ten Quick Comma Rules

(There are more comma rules but here are ten important ones for writers.)

Use commas to separate items in a list or series (words, phrases, and clauses).

Example: Colin enjoys *trains, cars,* and *Dr. Seuss.*

Use a comma after the words *ye" or no* when these are used to start a sentence.

Example: *Yes,* I would like some dessert.

Use a comma before and after a consecutive introductory prepositional phrase.

Example: *At the end of the day in Chicago*, people rush home from work.

Use a comma after an introductory participle or participial phrase.

Example: *Inspired by the professor's comments*, Ellie decided to go to law school.

Use a comma after an introductory adverb clause.

Example: *Before we boarded the airplane*, we needed to pass through security.

Use a comma to separate two or more adjectives that are placed before a noun.

Example: My Girl Scout troop is a *dedicated, kind* group.

Use a comma to separate independent clauses joined by the conjunctions *for, and, nor, but, or,* and *yet.*

Example: Troop 320 wanted to go camping, *but* it was too cold to sleep in tents.

Use a comma to cue a word or words in direct address.

Example: *Jim,* can you reach the top shelf?

Use a comma to cue a parenthetical expression like *such as, I believe,* and *for example.*

Example: This, *I believe,* is the best way to solve the problem.

Use a comma at the beginning and end of an appositive phrase.

Example: Susan, *my dear friend,* likes to kayak.

LESSON EIGHT: Commas, Part Two

Overview and Tips for Classroom Implementation

There are many rules for commas. This is one of the reasons why it is easy to make errors in comma usage. These five comma rules are the easier ones to master and remember.

Step-by-Step Lesson Instructions

Step One: Make copies of the *Five More Comma Rules* (see figure 4) for each student. The students can place a copy, for reference, in their writing folder or classroom notebook.

Step Two: Prior to the lesson, create *Comma Rule* envelopes for each pair of students with the following contents:

A complete set of the sentence strips (see figure 5)

10 commas (see figure 5)

Directions for the activity (see figure 5)

Step Three: Assign an envelope to a pair of students. Each student pair will "dump" the contents from the envelope and insert commas where needed for each sentence.

Additional Tips

Time the students for this activity. Five minutes should be plenty of time for the student pairs to complete this activity. It is also helpful for the students if the sentences are printed on different color paper. The commas are all printed on the same color paper that is different from the sentences. Using different colors helps the students to sort and categorize the information in this task.

Figure 4: FIVE MORE COMMA RULES

Use a comma after the salutation in a friendly letter.

Example: Dear Mom,

Use a comma after the closing in a friendly or business letter.

Example: Sincerely,

Use a comma to separate items in dates and addresses:

Example:

July 9, 2001

1600 Pennsylvania Ave.

Washington, D.C.

Use a comma to separate the speaker from the speaker's direct quotation.

Example:

"I need to ask you a question," Ellie said.

Use a comma after a mild interjection.

Example: Oh, you startled me.

Figure 5: Sentences, Commas and Directions

Directions: In this envelope there are ten sentences that need commas. Using your "Five More Comma Rule" reference sheet, insert commas where needed. Use the comma cards and place them in the location where the comma is needed in the following sentence.

,	,	,	,
,	,	,	,
,	,	,	,

Colin would like to go to the park but he needs to finish his homework.
Her birthday is on July 15 1998.
Tanisha can you open the window some more?
The band performed in Chicago New York London and Paris.
Our friends who are always thoughtful made us some cookies for the party.
More determined than ever the baseball player swung even harder.
Mr. King the well known author has another bestseller.
The long exhausting swim lesson finally finished.
"I moved from London to New York" the model explained.
The editor asked "Are you sure that you can meet the deadline?"

LESSON NINE: Comma Match

Overview and Tips for Classroom Implementation

This lesson provides continued practice and application of the comma rules. The students will work in teams to match the rules with the different examples.

Step-by-Step Lesson Instructions

Step One: Divide the class into groups of three to four students. Each student will need an envelope with the following:

Cards with each comma rule (see figure 6). Print these cards on light blue paper or card stock.

Cards with the examples (see figure 7). Print these cards on yellow paper or card stock.

You will need to make the envelopes for this activity before you conduct this lesson.

Step Two: Once the students have been divided into groups with three to four members, provide the following directions:

Match the reasons or rules for using a comma (these cards are light blue) with the examples. The examples are printed on yellow cards. You have five minutes to complete the activity.

In addition to providing these instructions verbally, be sure to write them down for the students on the chalkboard or on the envelopes that the students are using for this activity.

Step Three: As the students are working, be sure to circulate among the groups. This is always a great opportunity to clarify instructions and explain examples or rules for which the students have questions.

Additional Tips

Be sure to print the comma rules on color paper and the examples on a different colored paper. This helps the students to organize the information. In addition, it makes it easier for you to observe the students as they work on this activity as you circulate among the groups.

Figure 6: Comma Rules

Print these rules on light blue paper or card stock.

Comma should be placed after the salutation of a friendly letter.	Comma should be placed after the closing of a friendly or business letter.
Comma should be placed to separate items in dates and addresses.	Comma should be placed to separate the speaker from the quotation.
Comma should be placed to set off the consecutive introductory prepositional phrases.	Comma should be placed to separate a nonessential or nonrestrictive clause.
Comma should be placed to separate two or more adjectives that precede a noun.	Commas should be placed to separate independent clauses joined by a conjunction.
Comma should be placed to set off words in direct address.	Commas should be placed after an introductory participial phrase.

Figure 7: Comma Rules

Print these examples on light blue paper or card stock.

In the beginning of the day, the rooster crowed.	Ellie asked, "Can we go the Girl Scout meeting?"
Dear Jim,	Chased by the sheriff, the criminal surrendered.
An informed, trained representative will help you.	Very Truly Yours,
We completed the assignment, but it was not graded.	Colin, is that you in the drawing?
I was married on August 10, 1991.	These volunteers, who are going to the dinner later, are all members of the committee.

LESSON TEN: Common Nouns

Overview and Tips for Classroom Implementation

Nouns are one of the eight parts of speech. Common nouns begin with a small letter (or lowercase) and name a person, place, thing, or idea. Common nouns can be singular or plural.

Singular nouns name **one** person, place, thing, or idea. Plural nouns name **more than one** person, place, thing, or idea.

This activity introduces the characteristics of the common noun and provides practice for students to identify common nouns that are either singular or plural.

Step-by-Step Lesson Instructions

Step One: Before the lesson, you will need two large sheets of butcher paper. Label one sheet "Singular Common Nouns" and the other sheet will be labeled "Plural Common Nouns." You will also need a marker for each student in the class. Put one paper in the front of the classroom and the other paper in the back of the classroom.

Step Two: Review the following information about nouns with the students:

Nouns name a person, place, thing, or idea.

Common Nouns begin with a small (or lowercase) letter and can be either singular or plural.

Common Nouns are also nonspecific.

Singular Common Nouns name **one** person, place, thing or idea.

Example: person (student), place (classroom), thing (pencil) or idea (love).

Plural Common Nouns name **more than one** person, place, thing, or idea.

Example: person (students), place (classrooms), thing (pencils), and idea (loves).

Notice that you usually add *s* or *es* to make a common noun plural.

Step Three: Once you have reviewed the characteristics of common nouns, post two large sheets of butcher paper on each side of the classroom (one sheet of paper in the front of the classroom and one in the back). Divide the students into two groups. One group will be assigned to the "Singular Common Nouns" and one group will be assigned to the "Plural Common Nouns."

Step Four: Instruct the students to look around the classroom and identify as many common nouns as they can. When you say "go," the students are to write down, as fast as they can, any common nouns. The students that are assigned to the "Singular Common Nouns" write down only singular common nouns and the group assigned to the "Plural Common Nouns" should write down only the plural common nouns. Give the students about two minutes. Once time is called, have the groups switch positions. Repeat the activity.

Once the students have recorded common nouns at "Singular Common Nouns" and the "Plural Common Nouns" papers, review with the students the accuracy of their submissions.

Additional Tips

I always like to have the students check their work. Once the students have completed both posters, have each group check the answers for accuracy with your input. I also like to create a handout with all of their words with the information about common nouns as a reference for the students' writing folders.

LESSON ELEVEN: Connecting Clauses

Overview and Tips for Classroom Implementation

This lesson gives students the opportunity to practice using punctuation when combining clauses. This is a tricky writing skill for student writers. The students will review the basic rules for independent clauses and dependent clauses. Next, the students will participate in an activity that prompts them to connect clauses, using what they have learned from the "clause rules."

Step-by-Step Lesson Instructions

Step One: Prior to conducting the lesson, you will need the following:

Handouts for dependent and independent clauses (see figure 8). You will need enough copies for each student. The students can put these in their writing folders for future reference.

Using 4 x 6 index cards, divide each card into two pieces by cutting it so that each side has a unique shape and it connects only with that other card. In short, you are making two connecting puzzle pieces out of each index card.

Step Two: When the students enter the class, hand each student a puzzle piece. The students will find the classmate that matches their puzzle piece. Once the students have found their puzzle match, they are to sit together as partners for the mini lesson.

Step Three: Distribute the "Clause Rules" handout (see figure 8).

Using the examples on the "Clause Rules" handout, the students are to write sentences that join clauses with appropriate punctuation on the index cards. Since the students have two index card puzzles they are to write two sentences that use punctuation to connect clauses. The final product will look like this (see figure 9):

Figure 9: Sample Student Clause Puzzle

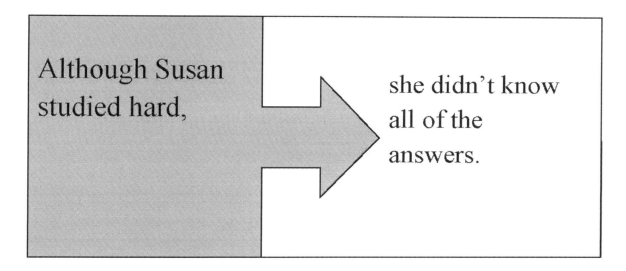

Additional Tips

I always collect the students' puzzle pieces and check for accuracy. The students' puzzle pieces are used for review in class the next day. The puzzle pieces are distributed and the students can review and practice the "Clauses Rules."

Figure 8: Clause Rules

Independent Clause

An independent clause is a group of words that contains a subject and a verb, and it expresses a complete thought. An independent clause can stand alone as a complete sentence.

Example: The dog ran to his bowl.

Dependent Clause

A dependent clause is a group of words that contains a subject and a verb, but it does not express a complete thought. **A dependent clause cannot be a sentence.**

Hint: A dependent clause often is marked by a dependent marker word. See the dependent marker word that is bolded in this example.

*Example: **When** the dog ran around the house*

A dependent marker word is a word added to the beginning of an independent clause that makes it into a dependent clause.

*Example: **When** the dog ran around the house, he grew tired.*

Some common dependent markers are: *after, although, as, as if, because, before, even if, even though, if, in order to, since, though, unless, until, whatever, when, whenever, whether,* and *while*.

Connecting Dependent and Independent Clauses

There are two types of words that can be used as connectors at the beginning of an independent clause: coordinating conjunctions and independent marker words.

Coordinating Conjunctions (FANBOYS)

The seven coordinating conjunctions used as connecting words at the beginning of an independent clause are <u>f</u>or, <u>a</u>nd, <u>n</u>or, <u>b</u>ut, <u>o</u>r, <u>y</u>et, <u>s</u>o. When the second independent clause in a sentence begins with a coordinating conjunction, a comma is needed before the coordinating conjunction.

Example: Simon worked hard to make it through the obstacle course, but it was not enough to get him to the top ranking for the race.

2. Dependent Marker Word

An independent marker word is a word used at the beginning of an independent clause. These words can always begin a sentence that can stand alone. When the second independent clause in a sentence has an independent marker word, a semicolon is needed before the independent marker word.

Some common independent markers are: *also, consequently, furthermore, however, moreover, nevertheless,* and *therefore.*

Example: Simon worked hard to make it through the obstacle course; **however,** it was not enough to get him to the top ranking for the race.

LESSON TWELVE: Dependent Clauses

Overview and Tips for Classroom Implementation

This is an advanced grammar mini lesson where students need to know the difference between independent and dependent clauses. Understanding this distinction supports the students' writing. This mini lesson will focus on indicators that will help students to identify the difference between independent and dependent clauses. The lesson will also demonstrate strategies that will allow students to turn a dependent clause into a complete thought.

Step-by-Step Lesson Instructions

Step One: Prior to conducting the lesson in class, create activity envelopes that contain the materials found in figure 10. Each envelope should contain a definition sheet and the dependent and independent clause strips.

Step Two: Divide the class into groups that contain three students each. Give an activity envelope to each student. Read the directions for the activity and instruct the students to begin. As the students work on the activity, circulate among the students to make sure that they are on task and to troubleshoot any questions or difficulties that the students might have with the task.

Step Three: Call time after five minutes and go over the answers as a large group.

Additional Tips

Be sure to paste the directions for the activity to the outside of the activity envelope. It is helpful for all students to have the directions given orally as well as written. You may also want to print the definition sheet on card stock and in a different color than the clause strips.

Figure 10: Materials for Lesson Twelve

Copy this page and cut out the Definitions for Independent and Dependent Clauses, the sentence strips, and activity directions. These materials should be placed in an envelope. You will need one envelope for each group of three students.

Definitions for Independent and Dependent Clauses

independent clause—a group of words that contains a subject and verb and expresses a complete thought. An independent clause is a sentence.

dependent clause—a group of words that contains a subject and verb but *does not* express a complete thought. A dependent clause *cannot* be a sentence. Often, a dependent clause is marked by a dependent marker word.

dependent marker word—a word added to the beginning of an independent clause that makes it into a dependent clause.

Examples: *after, although, as, as if, because, before, even if, even though, if, in order to, since, though, unless, until, whatever, when, whenever, whether, while*

Directions for Activity

When it is time to begin, the students will read the definitions of dependent and independent clauses, as well as dependent marker words.

Examine the clause strips and determine whether each is independent or dependent.

Once you have identified the dependent clauses, revise so that they are independent clauses that convey complete thoughts or ideas.

Clauses Strips—Duplicate and cut these out for the activity envelopes

Because the team won the game last week

As the actor exited the scene

Since I haven't been to the doctor

Colin acts like he has never seen a movie before.

Though I wanted to go to the exhibit

Everyone had a good time

Chocolate is delicious

Until the review board makes a decision about the student

He drove to the store

Whenever she goes to the grocery store

Even if he gets a raise

Even I can guess the answer

Although there is a secret passage

Although the map revealed a secret passage

I know that it is snowing outside

Maybe if it snows

LESSON THIRTEEN: End-Punctuation Marks

Overview and Tips for Classroom Implementation

This lesson is designed to review periods, question marks, and exclamation marks with students.

Step-by-Step Lesson Instructions

Step One: To prepare for the lesson, print enough copies of the accompanying handout (see figure 11) on card stock or heavy paper. From the handout, cut out the rules and examples for the period, question mark, and exclamation mark. Also cut out the sentences and activity directions from the handout (figure 11). Place each of these cutout items in an envelope.

Step Two: Divide the class into groups that contain three to four students. Give each group one of the envelopes and instruct the students to follow the directions for the activity (see figure 11).

Step Three: As the students work in groups, to complete the activity, circulate to answer any questions and to monitor progress. Once the students complete the activity, you can review the answers with the students through large group discussion.

Additional Tips

Print several copies of the handouts on different color paper so that the directions, rules, and examples can be different colors. When each lesson component is in a different color, it makes it easier for the students to sort and categorize the information.

Figure 11: Materials for Lesson 13

Directions: Cut out the directions, rules, and sentences and place into an envelope. You will need a complete set for each student group.

Activity Directions In this envelope is a set of rules for periods, question marks, and exclamation points. Examine each sentence and determine which end punctuation mark is needed. Using each of the rules as a header, place the sentences under the corresponding end punctuation mark rule.
Period Use a period at the end of a declarative sentence, a sentence that is a request, and one that includes a mild command. Use a period after abbreviations.
Question Mark Use a question mark at the end of a interrogative sentence.

Can you remember how many coins are in the collection

"I wish that I had something to give you," my sister said

Let's see what surprises are at the end of the story

Who has the answer to the request

Tell all of them to hurry up

Should the vegetables go in the refrigerator

I like that photo of you

Where are the photocopies for the project

Cool You can see all of the colors in the rainbow

LESSON FOURTEEN: Fragments and Run-Ons

Overview and Tips for Classroom Implementation

Sentence fragments and run ons are one of the most complex concepts to teach young writers. Be prepared to teach multiple lessons on sentence fragments and run ons to students. Give students as many opportunities to practice sentence fragment and run-on corrections. This lesson is designed to introduce sentence fragments and run ons.

Step-by-Step Lesson Instructions

Step One: Prior to the lesson, write the definitions for a sentence, fragment, and run-on sentence on large poster board. (The definitions are listed in Step Two.) Post each definition with the poster board in a different area of the classroom. Cut out the sentences, fragments, and run-on sentences from figure 12. You might need to make two sets for all of the students.

Step Two: **Review with students the following definitions:**

Sentence: A sentence can be a word (Go!) or a group of words that must contain a subject, verb, and a complete thought.

Fragment: A fragment is a group of words that might lack a subject or a verb and doesn't make a complete sentence.

Run On Sentence: A run-on sentence is two or more sentences that are incorrectly written as one sentence.

Step Three: Divide the students in pairs. Give each pair two sentences, fragments, or sentence run-ons from figure 12. Instruct the students to read the definition poster boards and match their sentence, fragment, or sentence run-on. You can give the students tape so that the strips of paper with the sentences, fragments, and run-ons can be attached to the correct corresponding definition poster board.

Step Four: Review the definitions and the students' posting of the sentences, fragments, and run-ons.

Additional Tips

It is always helpful to color code the strips of paper, (e.g., sentences are printed on green paper, sentence fragments are printed on pink, and the student run-ons are printed on yellow paper). You can also include examples of sentences, sentence fragments, and run-ons on each definition poster board.

Figure 12 Directions: Cut out each of the sentences, fragments, and run-ons.

Have you already eaten the ice cream?

At the beginning of the story.

Let's take the picture, we like the background for it.

Entering the interstate at the end of the trip.

Several clerks tried to help me finally I decided to leave.

During the party at the end of the holiday season.

I like to attend the baseball game.

I ate ice cream at the carnival.

The workers building the skyscraper are good they can finish the job in time.

Before they entered the contest.

After all of the applause for the audience.

I enjoyed the performance.

I need to get more information for the research report.

Please pass me the spices so I can finish making the pizza.

There are so many choices I can't make a decision.

LESSON FIFTEEN: *Further* vs. *Farther*

Overview and Tips for Classroom Implementation

Further and farther is often a confusing word pair for young writers. This activity provides students practice in determining when to use *further* and *farther*.

Step-by-Step Lesson Instructions

Step One: Review the following definitions for *further* and *farther* with the students.

<u>Farther</u> is used when discussing **distance.**

Examples:

I'm too tired to walk *farther*.

Ellie lives *farther* from my house than I thought.

<u>Further</u> is used to mean longer or more.

Example:

This position can go no *further*.

In Australia, the American dollar goes *further*.

I want to study Spanish *further*.

Step Two: Distribute two index cards to each student. One card should be labeled "further" and the other card should be labeled "farther."

Step Three: Display the practice sentences for the students (on an overhead projector, LCD projector, etc.). Show each sentence, one at a time, and ask the students to indicate if *further* or *farther* should be used by holding up the corresponding card.

Sample Sentences:

The boy shot the slingshot (farther/further) than I did.

The police officer waited for (farther/further) instructions.

Can you throw the ball any (farther/further)?

She lives (farther/further) from the school than I do.

The parents waited for (farther/further) information about the college acceptance.

Additional Tips

Once the students have responded to the sample sentences, the students can create their own sentences that use *further* and *farther*.

LESSON SIXTEEN: Homonyms

Overview and Tips for Classroom Implementation

Homonyms are sound-alike words that are easily confused. They are particularly troublesome for English language learners, and that is why it is important for us to explicitly teach homonyms.

Step-by-Step Lesson Instructions

Step One: Prior to the lesson, print the handout, "Common Homonyms" (see figure 13). Distribute a copy of the handout to each student. I always encourage the students to keep a copy in a folder that we use for writing.

Step Two: In preparation for the lesson, write the common homonyms listed on the handout (see figure 13). Write each word on a separate index card.

Step Three: Once you have distributed the Common Homonym handout and the homonym index card to each student, divide the students into groups of four to five students. Instruct the students that they need to create a tableaux for each homonym from the index cards.

Step Four: As the students present each homonym tableaux, the class can guess which homonym was represented.

Additional Tips

In order to speed up the pacing for the homonym tableaux, I always ask the groups to present each one in quick succession.

Figure 13: Common Homonyms

Common Homonyms

board/bored	brake/break	capital/capitol	choose/chose
desert/dessert	formally/formerly	hear/here	its/it's
loose/lose	quiet/quite	peace/piece	plain/plane
principal/principle	scene/seen	sweet/suite	there/their/they're
theirs/there's	throw/throe	threw/through	to/too/two
tow/toe	waist/waste	way/weigh	weak/week
wear/where	weather/whether	who's/whose	whirled/world
when/wend	witch/which	would/wood	your/you're

LESSON SEVENTEEN: Hyphens

Overview and Tips for Classroom Implementation

Hyphens are helpful punctuation marks that writers use to indicate to the reader when there are more syllables or connected words. Word processing has virtually eliminated the need to use hyphens to divide words into more than one syllable. Word processing programs keep words intact and automatically adjust spacing. However, we use the hyphen in English for words like, *father-in-law*. English also uses hyphens between two words that comprise a single adjective such as *good-natured*.

Step-by-Step Lesson Instructions

Step One: Review with students the following rules for hyphens:

Use a hyphen:

to syllabicate words at the end of a line when typing or writing.

to separate portions of certain compound words like *mother-in-law, sister-in-law,* or *brother-in-law.*

between two words that comprise a single adjective: *mean-spirited* or *happy-go-luckyStep Two:* Divide the group into student pairs. Give each pair of students a poster board or large sheet of construction paper. Instruct the students to create a poster that illustrates each of the three conditions for using a hyphen. The students can use the template in figure 14.

Figure 14: Hyphen Poster Template

Conditions to Use Hyphens
#1 State the rule, provide examples and illustration.
#2 State the rule, provide examples and illustration.

Additional Tips

It is important for students to create visuals that correspond with the different conditions for using hyphens in writing. The pairing of a strong visual with the hyphen rule supports students' understanding of the punctuation concept. Students can also create posters for each of the punctuation rules.

LESSON EIGHTEEN: Idiomatic Expressions Part One

Overview and Tips for Classroom Implementation

Idiomatic expressions are particularly problematic for English language learners because the meaning is implied, not directly stated. Most idiomatic expressions have cultural references that have been long forgotten, even by native English speakers.

Step-by-Step Lesson Instructions

Step One: You will need to photocopy (figure 15) for student handouts. The phrases listed on the handout are a sample of the many idiomatic expressions that are commonly used in American English.

Step Two: Distribute the handouts and ask the students to guess the meaning of each idiomatic expression. The students can work either independently or in pairs.

Step Three: Using a variety of sources, have the students verify the guess. An idiomatic dictionary and various websites (listed below) will help the students to verify the guess. Using the websites and reference books, have the students trace the origin of some of our more common idiomatic expressions.

Helpful websites include:

www.idiomsite.com

www.usingenglish.com/reference/idioms

www.yourdictionary.com

Step Four: Ask the students to share their answers, and how they created a definition for each idiomatic expression, with the class. Tally the students to see how many of their guesses were accurate.

Additional Tips

In addition to their completing the handout, I always like to have the students illustrate the idiomatic expressions. Visualization is essential for vocabulary internalization.

Figure 15: Idiomatic Expressions

Idiomatic Expressions

Directions: Guess the meaning of each of the following idiomatic expressions. Using a web search engine, look for websites like www.idiomsite.com or www.usingenglish.com/reference/idioms to verify each of your guesses. Also use these websites to discover the origin of these idiomatic expressions.

Idiomatic Expression	Guess the Meaning	Verify the Meaning	Origin of the Idiomatic Expression
A picture paints a thousand words			
Back seat driver			
Bad hair day			
Break a leg			
Chip on his shoulder			
Cut to the chase			
Diamond in the rough			
Face the music			
Houston, we have a problem			
Like a chicken without its head			
Nerd			
OK			
Pedal to the metal			
Play by ear			
Raining cats and dogs			

LESSON NINETEEN: Idiomatic Expressions Part Two

Overview and Tips for Classroom Implementation

Lesson Nineteen provides students with additional practice to learn about idiomatic expressions. Learning about idiomatic expressions is particularly useful for English language learners since the meaning is implied and not directly stated. Most idiomatic expressions have cultural references that have been long forgotten, even by native English speakers.

Step-by-Step Lesson Instructions

Step One: You will need to photocopy (figure 16) for student handouts. The phrases listed on the handout are a sample of the many idiomatic expressions that are commonly used in American English.

Distribute the handouts and ask the students to guess the meaning of each idiomatic expression. The students can work either independently or in pairs.

Step Two: Using a variety of sources, have the students verify the guess. An idiomatic dictionary and various websites (listed below) will help the students to verify the guess. Using the websites and reference books, have the students trace the origin of some of our more common idiomatic expressions.

Helpful websites include:

www.idiomsite.com

www.usingenglish.com/reference/idioms

www.yourdictionary.com

Step Three: Ask the students to share their answers with the class and how they created a definition for each idiomatic expression. Tally the students to see how many of their guesses were accurate.

Additional Tips

In addition to their completing the handout, I always like to have the students illustrate the idiomatic expressions. Visualization is essential for vocabulary internalization.

Figure 16: Idiomatic Expressions Part Two

Idiomatic Expressions

Directions: Guess the meaning of each of the following idiomatic expressions. Using a web search engine, look for websites like www.idiomsite.com or www.usingenglish.com/reference/idioms to verify each of your guesses. Also use these websites to discover the origin of these idiomatic expressions.

Idiomatic Expression	Guess the Meaning	Verify the Meaning	Origin of the Idiomatic Expression
Apple of my eye			
Back to square one			
None of your beeswax			
Brownie points			
Close, but no cigar			
Deadline			
Elvis has left the building			
Get out of bed on the wrong side			
Knock on wood			
Murphy's law			
Peeping Tom			
Shot in the dark			
Tongue in cheek			
Under the weather			
Wolf in sheep's clothing			

LESSON TWENTY: *Its* and *It's*

Overview and Tips for Classroom Implementation

I think there are many teachers who would agree that *its* and *it's* are often confused by students. As a writing teaching, I have taught the difference between *its* and *it's* multiple times. Here is a mini lesson to remind our students the difference between this commonly confused word pair.

Step-by-Step Lesson Instructions

Step One: Review with students the difference between *its* and *it's*.

it's is a contraction combining the words *it* and *is*

its is the possessive form of *it*.

Step Two: Distribute two index cards to each student and instruct them to write *its* on one card and *it's* on a second card.

Display the example sentences in figure 17 on an overhead or an LCD projector. As you display and read each sentence, have the students hold up the index card that provides the correct answer, either *its* or *it's*.

Additional Tips

I like to have the two index cards color-coded so when I am checking the students' responses, it is faster for me to determine if the correct answer is being displayed.

Figure 17: Practice Using its or it's

_____ (Its, It's) getting cold outside today.

I am learning how to play chess. _____ (Its, It's) a challenging game.

Let's portray _____ (its, it's) message more clearly.

I am thinking _____ (its, it's) owner should be contacted.

We know _____ (its, it's) hard to get the correct answer.

_____ (Its, It's) potential is difficult to determine at this time.

We are hoping _____ (its, it's) going to get easier to sell the house.

The team needs to work together in order to reach _____ (its, it's) full potential.

I like to bake cookies because _____ (its, it's) relaxing for me.

_____ (Its, It's) value is hard to determine in this volatile financial market.

LESSON TWENTY-ONE: Metaphorical Expressions

Overview and Tips for Classroom Implementation

The use of metaphors in writing can help authors to create pictures and images for the reader. Many words have both literal and figurative meanings. Literal meanings are most commonly used and metaphorical meanings can express meaning in a nonliteral way. Metaphors are powerful tools for expression and can help us explain and understand our world.

Using metaphors effectively can support students to develop more expressive writing.

Step-by-Step Lesson Instructions

Step One: Explain metaphor to the students.

A metaphor is an association or two objects by saying that one of them *is* the other.

A metaphor compares two objects, but does not use *like* or *as* or *than*.

A metaphor creates strong images and pictures for the audience.

Step Two: Discuss the following examples of metaphor:

My sister is a bear in the morning.

The stars are the flashlights of the night sky.

She has the heart of an angel.

Step Three: Divide the students into pairs.

Instruct the students to choose a famous person. The students should make a list of things (that aren't other people) to which a famous person could be compared.

Have the students create a list of metaphorical expressions for the famous person.

Additional Tips

You can have read the metaphors in class and have the students guess and identify the famous person.

LESSON TWENTY-TWO: Modifiers Are Dangling

Overview and Tips for Classroom Implementation

Students often create unclear statements in writing. Dangling modifiers are words or phrases that modify a word that is not clearly stated in the sentence. Modifiers describe, clarify, or give more detail about an idea or concept.

Step-by-Step Lesson Instructions

Step One: Explain the following examples to the students:

Example One: **Having prepared dinner, the radio was turned on.**

Having prepared states an action but it doesn't name the doer of this action. The doer must be the subject of the main clause that follows.

Having prepared dinner, Ellie turned the radio on.

Step Two: Discuss with the students the following strategies for correcting dangling modifiers:

Name the doer of the action in the main clause.

Change the phrase that dangles into a complete introductory clause by naming the doer of the action in that clause.

Step Three: Divide the students into pairs. Copy the examples (figure 18) of sentences with dangling modifiers and distribute to the student pairs. Have the students correct the examples.

Additional Tips

As an extension activity, ask the students to create sentences with dangling modifiers that need to be corrected.

Figure 18: Practice Correcting Sentences with Dangling Modifiers

Practice Correcting Sentences with Dangling Modifiers

After reading the book, the ending was not satisfying.

Leaving for the next train, your trip should be fine.

The experiment was a success, not having followed correct procedures.

After getting the job, the work was not satisfying.

Once I left for the office, it started to rain.

Knowing what the outcome might be, the movie was not enjoyable.

Suggested Revisions

After reading the book, I thought that ending was not satisfying.

Leaving for the next train, you should be able to have a fine trip.

Their experiment was a success, not having followed correct procedures.

After getting the job, I thought that the work was not satisfying.

Once I left for the office, I noticed that it started to rain.

Knowing what the outcome might be, I thought that the movie was not enjoyable.

LESSON TWENTY-THREE: Onomatopoeia

Overview and Tips for Classroom Implementation

Onomatopoeia is a figure of which imitates the word that it represents. Writers like Edgar Allen Poe are well known for the masterful use of onomatopoeia in poems like "The Bells."

Step-by-Step Lesson Instructions

Step One: Have students watch the following videos which introduce and explain onomatopoeia.

http://www.youtube.com/watch?v=q-BVwwKTjlI

and

http://www.youtube.com/watch?v=evUzS6K-5Wg&feature=related

Step Two: Prior to this lesson, I collect a variety of toys that often come with kids' meals, or windup toys. Put the toys in a box prior to conducting the lesson in class. Divide the students into pairs and ask each pair of students to select a toy.

Step Three: Give the students two minutes to brainstorm words that they could use to describe the toy's sounds. Once the students have a list of words, invite them to write a sentence that contains onomatopoeia.

Additional Tips

Using onomatopoeia, the students can create a brief four- to six-line-poem about their toy .

LESSON TWENTY-FOUR: Placing Prepositions

Overview and Tips for Classroom Implementation

When students understand how to identify and use prepositions in writing, they become more skilled in adding spatial and temporal detail in writing.

Step-by-Step Lesson Instructions

Step One: Divide the students into pairs. For this mini lesson, you will need a small toy car and a small cutout of a person for each student pair. Give each student pair a car and person cutout.

Step Two: Give the students an explanation and demonstration of the relationship between the cutout person and the toy car. For example, the person can be "on top of the car" or "in the car." Instruct the students to write as many statements, in present tense, about the cutout person and the car. Give the students about five minutes to create and state as many relationships as possible between the cutout person and the toy car.

Step Three: Give the students the list of common prepositions (see figure 19). Instruct the students to review the list and to identify how many prepositions that they used.

Step Four: In a large class discussion, discuss what prepositions do in language and for our writing. Be sure to include the following:

Prepositions…

Signal and introduce the answer to the questions, *Where? When?* and *How?*

How can prepositions change the meaning of a sentence?

Additional Tips

You could give the students a two-column graphic organizer to document the sentences. The first column would prompt the students to record their sentences. The second column would prompt the students to identify and list the prepositions that the students used.

Figure 19: Commonly Used Prepositions

Commonly Used Prepositions

aboard	about	above	across	after
against	along	amid	among	anti
around	as	at	before	behind
below	beneath	beside	besides	between
beyond	but	by	concerning	considering
despite	down	during	except	excepting
excluding	following	for	from	in
inside	intro	like	minus	near
of	off	on	onto	opposite
outside	over	past	per	plus
regarding	round	save	since	than
through	to	toward	towards	under
underneath	unlike	until	up	upon
versus	via	with	within	without

LESSON TWENTY-FIVE: Prefix Carousel

Overview and Tips for Classroom Implementation

This mini lesson is designed for students to become more familiar with prefix meanings. This lesson also gives students the opportunity to brainstorm and think about word creation.

Step-by-Step Lesson Instructions

Step One: Create posters with the prefixes from figure 20. Write the prefix and meaning on each poster board. For a class of about twenty-five students, it is good to have at least ten poster boards with prefixes.

Step Two: Post the poster boards with prefixes around the classroom. Divide the students into groups of three. Instruct the students that they are to write down as many words that they can think of, using the prefix listed on the poster board, in thirty seconds. It is helpful to use a timer to keep students on task and focused. When the thirty seconds are up, instruct the students to move to the next poster board. Instruct the students to look at the words on the new poster board and direct them to add to the previous group's list. Give the students thirty seconds to add more words on the poster board with the corresponding prefix.

Step Three: Continue to have the groups of students move from one poster board prefix location to another every thirty seconds until they have contributed to each list.

Additional Tips

When the students are working on the last four or five prefix poster boards, I allow them to use dictionaries because it becomes increasingly challenging to generate more words for the lists. It is also helpful to increase the time at each station as the students progress through the groups.

Figure 20: Prefixes

Prefix	Meaning	Word Examples
anti	against	antifreeze
de	opposite	defrost
dis	not, opposite of	disembark
en, em	cause to	enforce, embrace
in, im	in	infield
in, im	not	injustice, impossible
inter	between	interplay
mid	middle	midway
mis	wrongly	misinform
non	not	nonsense
over	over	overpass
pre	before	prefix, preview
re	again	rerun
semi	half	semitransparent
sub	under	subway
super	above	supernova
trans	across	transport
un	not	unfriendly

LESSON TWENTY-SIX: Prefix Puzzle

Overview and Tips for Classroom Implementation

This mini lesson is intended to develop students' understanding of prefixes.

Step-by-Step Lesson Instructions

Step One: Prior to the lesson, you will need enough copies of the prefix graphic organizer for each group of students, and five different colors of construction paper. Each prefix group should be a different color, with the puzzle pieces either photocopied or written onto them.

Group 1: Copy onto blue paper the puzzle pieces with divided words to demonstrate the prefix *sub*.

sub	way
sub	marine

Group 2: Copy onto red paper the puzzle pieces with divided words to demonstrate the prefix *pre*.

pre	view
pre	sent

Group 3: Copy onto green paper the puzzle pieces with divided words to demonstrate the prefix *mis*.

mis	take
mis	understand

Group 4: Copy onto yellow paper the puzzle pieces with divided words to demonstrate the prefix *inter*.

inter	play
inter	view

Step Two: Cut up each sheet. All of the puzzle pieces should be separated. Put all of the puzzle pieces in a large envelope.

Step Three: Divide the class into groups of three students. Give each group all of the prefix puzzle pieces and a copy of the prefix graphic organizer.

Step Four: Instruct the students to put the puzzle pieces together, matching the divided words. Once the students have correctly assembled the puzzle pieces, they can complete the prefix graphic organizer (see figure 21).

Additional Tips

Once the students have completed the prefix graphic organizer, I like to have a large group discussion about the words. I ask the students if they notice any patterns and what they may have learned about the different prefixes. We make a chart together, recording what they have learned about prefixes and any additional observations that they made about language.

Figure 21: Prefix Puzzle Organizer

Prefix Puzzle Organizer

Prefix	Prefix Meaning	Words	More words with the same prefix
sub			
pre			
mis			
inter			

LESSON TWENTY-SEVEN: Pronouns: Gender Impact

Overview and Tips for Classroom Implementation

My high school students were always surprised when I explained how gender pronouns functioned in Standard English. This mini lesson is designed to increase student awareness of gender and language through the study of pronouns.

Step-by-Step Lesson Instructions

Step One: Have the students select a character from this list:

Cowboy, teacher, rock star, nurse, doctor, or lawyer

Once the students have selected a character, have them write a story about the character. Give the students twenty minutes to draft a one- to two-paragraph narrative story about the selected character.

Step Two: Divide the students into pairs. With the student's partner, instruct the students to circle the pronouns that are used to describe the selected character. Ask the students to answer the following questions:

What is the gender of the character?

How do you know the gender of the character (indicated by what pronouns were assigned)?

Step Three: Ask the students to share the answers to the questions in Step Two as part of a large group discussion. Discuss with the students how pronouns can impact the reader's assumptions about a text. You can make a table with the characters like the one below and tally the students' gender assignments.

Additional Tips

The following resource offers tips for avoiding gender-biased language in writing.

http://owl.english.purdue.edu/owl/resource/608/01/

Figure 22: Pronouns and Gender

Character	Pronouns Associated with the Character	Female or Male?
cowboy		
teacher		
rock star		
nurse		
doctor		
lawyer		

LESSON TWENTY-EIGHT: Proper Nouns

Overview and Tips for Classroom Implementation

Since there are several types of nouns, student writers need to understand how they differ. Student writers do make frequent errors in capitalization that are often the result of not knowing and understanding what designates a proper noun. This lesson reviews the characteristics of proper nouns and provides practice for the students.

Step-by-Step Lesson Instructions

Step One: Obtain a box or large bag. Collect a variety of items. that could be designated as a proper noun. For example, a map with the country, city, or location circled; pictures of famous people; photos of famous buildings; small toy cars; or excerpts from famous documents or texts. Put about twenty to thirty items in the bags.

Step Two: Using figure 23, review the characteristics of proper nouns and explain why these words are capitalized.

Step Three: Circulate among the students and invite them to draw an item from the box or bag that you created. When a student takes out an item—let's say for this example that it's a map with a city circled—instruct the student to show the item to the class. Next, the students should identify the proper noun. In this example, it's the name of a city, and why it is a proper noun and should be capitalized. Repeat this procedure until the items have all been selected.

Additional Tips

Keep the rules and criteria for proper nouns posted as you and the students go through the items. The students can use the list (figure 23) as a reference throughout the activity. Posting the list supports visual learners and students who have challenges with processing.

Figure 23: Proper Nouns

Proper Nouns

Proper nouns, like other nouns, name a person, place, thing, or idea. However, proper nouns further distinguish nouns since they name or label a particular entity, unlike common nouns.

Proper nouns are capitalized.

Proper nouns are not usually preceded by an article (*a, an, the*).

Proper nouns (the names of specific people, places, organizations, and sometimes things). Here are some examples:

President Obama

Chicago, Illinois

National Council of Teachers of English

Toyota Prius

LESSON TWENTY-NINE: More Pronoun Practice

Overview and Tips for Classroom Implementation

Students often forget to identify the antecedent when using pronouns in writing. As a result, the reader can become easily confused when the pronoun does not have an easily understood referent.

Step-by-Step Lesson Instructions

Step One: Review with students the relationship between pronouns and antecedents.

Pronouns take the place of a noun and refer to the noun which it replaces.

The correct pronouns must be used so that the reader clearly understands which noun your pronoun is referring to.

Step Two: You can either make copies of figure 24 or display it on an overhead projector. The students can work in pairs or the class can work through the activity as a whole-group instruction.

Step Three: Have the students read the passage in figure 24. The students will notice that pronouns are missing in the passage. Instruct the students to insert appropriate pronouns where they are missing. Once the pronouns are inserted, instruct the students to identify the antecedent for each pronoun.

Additional Tips

It is helpful to color-code the pronouns and the antecedent so that these are more obvious to the student.

Figure 24: Pronoun Practice

Pronoun Practice

Susan decided that _____ needed some special ingredients for the dinner that _____ was making for _____ family. _____ grabbed her purse and headed to the grocery store. At the grocery store, _____ noticed that it was very crowded. Many customers were walking down the aisles and filling _____ carts with groceries. Since Susan was in a hurry, _____ decided to grab a basket, instead of a cart, and dashed down one of the aisles.

LESSON THIRTY: Pronouns: Possessive

Overview and Tips for Classroom Implementation

A pronoun used to demonstrate possession is called a possessive pronoun. Students are often confused when to use the masculine, feminine, or neuter form of possessive pronouns in Standard English. This lesson allows students to practice with the different possessive pronouns.

Step-by-Step Lesson Instructions

Step One: Review the possessive pronouns with the students:

mine, yours, his, hers, its, ours, yours, and *theirs*

As illustrated in the following examples, possessive pronouns demonstrate relationships.

It is *mine*.

First person pronoun, *mine,* refers to the speaker.

No, it is not *yours*.

Second person pronoun, *yours*, refers to the person being spoken to (you).

Maybe it is *hers*.

Third person pronoun, *hers,* reefs to the person being spoken about (she).

I know *its* behavior seems odd.

Third person pronoun, *its,* refers to an object, not a person.

Step Two: Once you have reviewed possessive pronouns with the students, ask the students to create sentences like those in your examples. The students can work in pairs to create the sentences. It should take about five minutes for the students to create sample sentences for each of the possessive pronouns.

Step Three: Instruct the students to select three of the sample sentences that they created. Next, the students will illustrate the relationship of each possessive pronoun.

Give the students about ten minutes to complete these steps.

Additional Tips

When the students illustrate the possessive pronoun relationships, they can do so in a variety of formats. I have successfully used all of the following:

- Bring large butcher block paper and tape it to a wall in the classroom. The students can create their illustrations on large butcher block paper.

- Distribute card stock and have one sample possessive pronoun on each paper.

- If you have access to computers in your classroom, use a drawing program for the students to create the possessive pronoun illustrations digitally.

LESSON THIRTY-ONE: Quotation Marks Part One

Overview and Tips for Classroom Implementation

There are many rules which students most know and remember when using quotations in writing. The next group of lessons examines how quotation marks are used in a variety of circumstances.

Step-by-Step Lesson Instructions

Step One: Students are often confused about when to underline or italicize a title or when they need to use quotations. Quotation marks are used to punctuate titles when it is a part of a longer work. For example, articles are part of a larger text, like a newspaper or magazine. Poems and essays are usually part of a larger volume or collection of poems and essays. Song titles are usually part of an artist's compact disc or playlist. When I begin this lesson, I explain that titles are in quotation marks when they are part of a larger work.

Step Two: To illustrate this concept, I have created enough envelopes with copies of pre-selected titles.

I divide the students into groups of three to four students. The students are instructed to examine each of the titles from their envelopes and decide whether the title should be underlined (or italicized) or punctuated with quotation marks. Give the students about five minutes to complete this activity.

Step Three: Once the students have determined how a title should be punctuated, review the responses with the students as a large-group activity.

Additional Tips

For further practice and assessment, invite the students to create lists of titles that their classmates can punctuate.

LESSON THIRTY-TWO: Quotation Marks Part Two

Overview and Tips for Classroom Implementation

This mini lesson will focus on the situations on which quotation marks are needed. The students will work in collaborative groups to identify and list the reasons for using quotation marks in writing.

Step-by-Step Lesson Instructions

Step One: Divide the students into groups of three members.

Step Two: Introduce quotation marks and how these punctuation marks indicate the direct words that someone speaks. The open and close quotation marks indicate the beginning and end of the actual words of the speaker. In a large group discuss the following examples:

Quotation examples:

Example: Ellie is often described as "compassionate" and "caring."

1. *Reason for Quotation:* To highlight key words, phrases, and sentences.

Example: The columnist wrote in the school newspaper, "The lunch program must improve. If the school administration is truly concerned about student health and obesity, better food that is not heavily processed must be served."

2. *Reason for Quotation:* A direct quote is written from a text.

Example: The student newspaper columnist asked Principal Smith, "What efforts have been made to improved the quality of school cafeteria food?"

3. *Reason for Quotation:* A direct quote of a statement or question.

Step Three: Once you have reviewed the examples and reasons for quotation marks, instruct the students to write at least three examples for each of the three "reasons for quotations." It should take the students about five minutes to compose the sentences.

Step Four: Instruct the students to exchange their sentences with another group. Once the students have received the sentences from another group, instruct each student group to identify the "reason for quotation." As the students are working, the teacher should be circulating among the students, checking and answering questions. This step should take five minutes.

Additional Tips

A three-column graphic organizer, using each "reason for quotation" as the header for each column, can be used to facilitate *Step Four*. The students can record the sentences that they received from the other group under the appropriate header in the three-column graphic organizer.

LESSON THIRTY-THREE: Semicolon

Overview and Tips for Classroom Implementation

Most student writers do not use the semicolon, largely because they don't have enough experience with this punctuation mark. The semicolon is a wonderful tool for writers in that it is a powerful rhetorical tool. In this lesson, the students will learn about the three semicolon rules through "real" text examples.

Step-by-Step Lesson Instructions

Step One: Prior to teaching this lesson, select a strong rhetorical text to use for this lesson. Here are some suggestions:

"Letter from Birmingham Jail"

"A Modest Proposal"

Hillary Clinton's Speech on Women's Rights

(Link to video and text: http://www.americanrhetoric.com/speeches/hillaryclintonbeijingspeech.htm)

Step Two: Students can work in pairs or alone. Give the students the text that you selected for this lesson and direct them to highlight or circle all of the semicolons that are in the text.

Step Three: Have the students complete the following graphic organizer:

Figure 23: Semicolon Practice

Semicolon Practice

Passage That Contains a Semicolon	Why do you think the author use a semicolon rather than a weaker punctuation mark like a comma?	How does the semicolon affect how you read the passage?

Step Four: Next, give the students a version of the selected passage where all of the semicolons were removed. Ask the students: How are the versions different? How does the author's use of the semicolon affect the meaning and emphasis?

Step Five: Make a copy of figure 24. Review with the students the rules for semicolons.

Figure 24: Semicolon Uses

Semicolon Uses

Use a semicolon to join independent clauses when the two clauses should have equal emphasis:

Airplane traffic slowed to a standstill; the tarmac was congested with planes.

Use a semicolon to join items in a series when the individual elements already include commas:

The largest cities in the United States include: New York, New York; Chicago, IL; Los Angelos, CA.

Additional Tips

You can also share the following video clip from the Online Writing Lab (OWL) at Purdue University to review semicolons: http://www.youtube.com/user/OWLPurdue.

Once the students have a better understanding of semicolons, they can practice on their own writing draft.

LESSON THIRTY-FOUR: Sentence Fragments

Overview and Tips for Classroom Implementation

This lesson is designed for students to identify and revise sentence fragments. Sentence fragments and sentence run-ons are difficult for students to understand because they require writers to apply everything that they know and understand about grammar and sentence structure.

Step-by-Step Lesson Instructions

Step One: Prior to conducting the lesson in class, print enough copies of figure 25 for each group of students. I suggest having the students work in pairs or in groups of no more than four students. Cut out the sentence strips from figure 25 and place them in an envelope for each student.

Step Two: Provide some sample sentence fragments and discuss with your students the following questions and brainstorm answers:

What makes a sentence fragment a sentence fragment?

As you look at the sample sentence fragments, ask yourself, What's missing? What information do I need after reading this sentence fragment? How can I add information so that I can create a sentence that has a complete meaning?

Tip: You might want to point out that sentence fragments are ineffective writing because they create confusion for the reader.

Step Three: Divide the students into pairs or groups of no more than four students. Distribute the sentence strip envelopes that were cut out from figure 25. Direct the students to do the following.

Take the strips out of the envelope. Combine two strips to create a complete sentence. Add punctuation and capitalization to form a complete sentence.

Figure 25: Phrase Strips

I could eat
a large plate of spaghetti
for lunch
My grandmother loves to tell
me stories
about her life on the farm
Her little sister loves to play
with dolls
nearly every day
Would someone like to
make some delicious chocolate cake
for my upcoming birthday
My favorite music
is featured
on this great website

Step Four: Once the students have created the completed sentences, they can submit them for evaluation. The students can also share their sentences as a whole group. Whichever method you choose, discuss how the students revised the strips to create complete coherent sentences.

Additional Tips

The students can create sentence fragment strips for another round of practice. These newly created sentence fragment strips can be exchanged with other student groups. I also suggest that the students can record the sentences that they create to share and discuss as a whole group.

LESSON THIRTY-FIVE: Spelling Words That Challenge Us

Overview and Tips for Classroom Implementation

Despite spell-check, there are words that are challenging for students to spell correctly. This lesson provides practice for students to spell some of the most challenging words.

Step-by-Step Lesson Instructions

Step One: Prior to the lesson, make a copy of figure 26 for the students.

Step Two: Distribute figure 26 for the students and instruct them to identify which words are tricky to spell. Have the students record the tricky words in a two-column organizer and add a trick or strategy to help them remember how to spell it in the future (see figure 27).

Additional Tips

Once the students start this personal spelling list, they can continue to add to the list throughout the school year.

Figure 26: Words That Are Tricky to Spell

absence	defendant	height	manipulate	sergeant
accidentally	definite	heiress	mileage	sizable
acquaint	dilemma	heredity	miniscule	success
acquire	discipline	humane	misspell	symbolize
aerial	eighth	icicle	neighbor	symmetry
analysis	emigrate	ideally	niceties	tendency
analyze	emphasis	immature	nickel	thorough
apparent	exceed	immigrate	niece	through
appearance	excessive	interfere	nominal	thwart
belief	existence	interrupt	nonentity	tonal
believe	flabbergast	irregular	occurred	tragedy
bureau	fractious	jaunty	occurrence	truly
calendar	gauge	jealous	omnipotent	unified
catastrophe	genuine	justification	operable	unique
category	grateful	knowledge	paradigm	unnecessary
cemetery	gratitude	liberal	persuasive	usually
changeable	grisly	license	possess	vicious
column	guarantee	likelihood	regrettable	villain
committed	guilty	lonely	reliance	violin
condemn	handkerchief	loveable	rhythm	weird
conscience	handsome	luxury	secede	wield
conscious	handedly	mammoth	seize	yield
courageous	handwritten	manageable	separate	zealous

Figure 27: Tricky Spelling Words

Personal Spelling Dictionary

WORD LIST	HOW I CAN REMEMBER TO SPELL IT

LESSON THIRTY-SIX: Subject and Verb Agreement

Overview and Tips for Classroom Implementation

We learn grammar best through authentic language experiences. Our students can find grammar whenever they engage in language experiences. This lesson teaches students about sentence and verb agreement through authentic language experiences. The students will explore authentic texts such as song lyrics and newspapers, and identify correct and incorrect uses and examples of subject and verb agreement.

Step-by-Step Lesson Instructions

Step One: Review subject-verb agreement. Discuss how subject-verb changes in various forms of written text and the effect that it has on the content.

Step Two: Instruct the students to go to the website of a local newspaper and have the students select two to three headlines that grab their attention. Instruct the students to find the subject and verb in each headline. The students might have some difficulty finding the subject and verb and determining if there is agreement in the headline. If they do, be sure to discuss and assist the students.

Step Three: Next, select several sentences from a variety of novels. Distribute the sentence samples and instruct the students to identify the subject and verb. Have the students determine if the subject and verb in each sentence agrees.

Additional Tips

Once the students have identified subjects and verbs in a variety of texts and determined whether there is agreement, have them take a practice quiz. There are some great resources for subject-verb agreement and sample quizzes at The Purdue Online Writing Lab:

http://owl.english.purdue.edu/owl/resource/599/01/.

LESSON THIRTY-SEVEN: Writer's Proofreading Checklist

Overview and Tips for Classroom Implementation

Student writers need tools that support them to evaluate and proofread their own writing. This lesson incorporates a graphic organizer that student writers can use to proofread.

Step-by-Step Lesson Instructions

Step One: Remind your students about proofreading and why it is important. I always remind my students that proofreading is important because word processing programs do not catch all of the errors. I also share that in addition to checking grammar, spelling, and punctuation, they are also making sure that the content is coherent.

Step Two: Make enough copies of the *Writer's Proofreading Checklist* (figure 28) for each student. Go over the content of the proofreading checklist with the students.

Additional Tips

Have the students place a copy of the *Writer's Proofreading Checklist* in their writing notebook or folder.

Figure 28: Writer's Proofreading Checklist

Writer's Proofreading Checklist

Name:	
Title of Piece:	
Proofreading Reminder	Comments
VERB TENSE is used logically and consistently.	
PASSIVE VOICE is not past tense and it is usually vague and informative.	
THIRD PERSON for formal writing, it is best to write in third person.	
SLANG and **COLOQUIALISMS** should be avoided. A reader who is unfamiliar with these phrases may be confused.	
TRICKY WORDS AND PHRASES LIKE: a lot and you know should be avoided in formal writing. Watch out for confusing words like: it's and its affect and effect accept and except lead and led.	

LESSON THIRTY-EIGHT: *Very*

Overview and Tips for Classroom Implementation

I developed this lesson when it seemed to me that every student in my classes use the word *very* at least ten times in every written assignment (this is also true for *a lot*).

Step-by-Step Lesson Instructions

Step One: Photocopy the "Very" Handout (see figure 29). Give each student a copy of the handout and explain to the students that the word *very* is overused and should be avoided in our writing, since it is not effective.

Step Two: Divide the students into pairs and distribute the handout (figure 29).

Step Three: Instruct the students to write a one-word equivalent for each of the "very" expressions.

Step Four: When the students have completed the handout, go over the answers in a large group.

Additional Tips

The students can create additional "very" expressions and create quizzes for each other for additional practice.

Figure 29: "Very" Expressions

"Very" Expressions

"Very" Expressions	One Word Equivalent
very painful	
very stormy	
very happy	
very lonely	
very sad	
very indifferent	
very knowledgeable	
very dry	
very wet	
very soon	
very infrequent	
very hopeless	
very sweet	
very salty	
very knowledgeable	
very clear	
very confusing	
very ashamed	

LESSON THIRTY-NINE:
Words That Are Confusing

Overview and Tips for Classroom Implementation

Homonyms, or sound-alike words, can be can be confusing for students. English language learners and native speakers often confuse sound-alike words in their writing, resulting in an incorrect word choice.

Step-by-Step Lesson Instructions

Step One: Prior to the lesson, write each word of the sound-alike words on separate index cards. You should have one word card per student (see figure 30).

Step Two: I always like to pass out the cards to the students as they enter the class. Once each student has one of the *sound alike word cards*, instruct them to find the student with the matching sound-alike word. For example, the student with "board" written on their card needs to find the student with the word "bored."

Step Three: Once the students find their *sound-alike word* partner, they will work in pairs to provide a brief explanation of why the words are different. The students will share their explanations as a large group.

Additional Tips

As an extension activity, I like to have the students create posters that explain how the sound-alike words are different. The students also provide pictures, drawings, and cartoons to visualize the difference between the words.

Figure 30: Sound-Alike Word Pairs

board bored	brake break
capital capitol	choose chose
desert dessert	formally formerly
hear here	its it's
loose lose	quiet quite
peace piece	plain plane
principal principle	their there they're
theirs there's	to to two
threw through	waist waste
weather whether	who's whose

LESSON FORTY: *Your* and *You're*

Overview and Tips for Classroom Implementation

Your and *you're* are commonly confused words. This lessons reviews the difference between *your* and *you're*.

Step-by-Step Lesson Instructions

Step One: Show the students this video clip and explain and demonstrate the difference between *your* and *you're*.

The first clip is from the television show *Friends:*

http://www.youryoure.com/

Step Two: Once the students have viewed the clip, summarize the difference between *your* and *you're*.

your is a possessive adjective, indicating ownership of something

That is **your** friend.

Where is **your** notebook?

you're is a contraction (combination) of **you** and **are**

Do you know what **you're** saying?

You're a great friend.

Additional Tips

The following website includes songs about punctuation and grammar. The multimodal approach in the teaching of grammar supports students' understanding of language.

http://www.educationalrap.com/song/dots-and-dashes-punctuation.html

ABOUT THE AUTHOR

Katie began her career in education as a high school English teacher and taught mainly in the Chicago Public Schools over twenty years ago. She went on to earn her Ph.D. in education and is now an associate professor of secondary education at National Louis University and an onsite professional development consultant for the National Council of Teachers of English (NCTE). Her work with NCTE has provided her the opportunity to work in schools all over the country, including rural, urban, and suburban locations. These school experiences provide Katie with a rich context in which to address the issues that challenge literacy educators today.

Currently Katie's research focuses on differentiated instruction in the English language arts classroom, school reform, and creating rigorous literacy learning experiences for all students in the twenty-first century. Katie frequently publishes in journals and is a presenter at professional conferences. Her authored book titles include: *The Teacher's Big Book of Graphic Organizers* and *The English Teacher Survivial Guide 2nd Ed.*

Visit her website at www.KatherineMcKnight.com